The Prayer of
St. Ephrem the Syrian

Books by William C. Mills

Pastoral Ministry

Church, World, and Kingdom: The Eucharistic Foundations of Alexander Schmemann's Pastoral Theology

Kyprian Kern: Orthodox Pastoral Service

Called to Serve: Readings on Ministry From the Orthodox Church

Church and World: Essays in Honor of Michael Plekon

Biblical Prayer and Spirituality

A 30 Day Retreat: A Personal Guide to Spiritual Renewal

Walking with God: Stories of Life and Faith

Come Follow Me

The Prayer of St. Ephrem: A Biblical Commentary

Our Father: A Prayer for Christian Living

Encountering Jesus in the Gospels

Lectionary Series

A Light to the Gentiles: Reflections on the Gospel of Luke

Baptize All Nations: Reflections on the Gospel of Matthew for the Pentecostal Season

Feasts of Faith: Reflections on the Major Feast Days

From Pascha to Pentecost: Reflections on the Gospel of John

Let Us Attend: Reflections on the Gospel of Mark for the Lenten Season

Prepare O Bethlehem: Reflections on the Scripture Readings for the Christmas-Epiphany Season

THE PRAYER OF
ST. EPHREM THE SYRIAN

A Biblical Commentary

William C. Mills

First Published by Orthodox Research Institute, 2008
Reprinted by OCABS Press, 2018

ISBN 1-60191-043-6 (Paperback)

ST. EPHREM THE SYRIAN
January 28

By a flood of tears you made the desert fertile
And your longing for God brought forth fruits in abundance
By the radiance of miracles you illumined the whole universe
Our Father Ephrem pray to Christ God to Save our souls!

(Troparion)

Ever anticipating the hour of judgment
You learned lamented bitterly venerable Ephrem
Through your deeds you were a teacher by example
Therefore universal Father, you rouse the slothful to repentance

(Kontakion)

For

Father Ramon J. Gonzalez

TABLE OF CONTENTS

INTRODUCTION

Not much is known about the early life of St. Ephrem the Syrian.[1] He was born in 306 somewhere near the city of Nisbis (now known as Nusaybin), which is located in modern day Syria. Tradition states that Ephrem was raised in a pagan household and then as an adult was baptized and received into the Christian faith. However, we are not really sure when Ephrem became a Christian. Nisbis was located near the Euphrates River and had a diverse ethnic and religious population. By the time of Ephrem's birth, the area was already settled and was a multicultural and ethnic center; a trade route between East and West.

Ephrem was ordained to the diaconate by Bishop Jacob who was one of the 318 bishops who attended the council at Nicea in 325 AD. Later Ephrem went to live in Edessa, which is now modern day Iraq. As a deacon, Ephrem was allowed to preach during

---

[1] Sometimes his name is spelled St. Ephraim or Ephraem.

the liturgical services. According to later writers, we know that Ephrem was a very good preacher and teacher of the faith. Jerome, who lived in the fourth century, described Ephrem as follows: "Ephrem, a deacon of the Church of Edessa, wrote a great deal in the Syriac language. He attained such distinction that his writings are read in some churches after the scriptural lections. I have a read a work of his on the Holy Spirit, which someone had translated from Syriac into Greek, and even in translation, I could recognize the acumen of a lofty intellect." We also know from the writings of Palladius and Theodore the Studite that Ephrem was an important figure in the Church. Ephrem was never ordained to the priesthood, but this did not prevent him from fulfilling his ministry in the Church. The liturgical hymns in honor of Ephrem draw on his own work in the Church as a poet and defender of the Christian faith and proclaimer of the Gospel:

> You beheld the good things of Paradise
> And delighted richly in the incorruptible gardens blooming there!
> You yourself blossomed forth divine reason to the world.
> Venerable one, as we commune with this in spiritual love,
> Let us also spiritually grow in our souls.
> With streams of tears you wrote of the coming of the Judge!
> You taught all to kindle the lamps of the soul,

Crying out that when the Bridegroom comes,
All should be robed in bright garments,
And go forth to meet the Bridegroom, Christ!

You surrounded the flesh with the protection of
abstinence, Father,
And with prayer and vigil,
You mortified the movement of the passions.
Therefore the power of the Spirit dwelt within you,
Revealing your spiritually to be a universal lamp.
("Lord I Call" *verses for the feast of St. Ephrem*)

You watered your bed with tears, as the Prophet
said,
And sought repentance through the lessons of life.
You showed us through your words the fear of
judgment by deeds!
As we gather together in honor of your memo-
ry, all-blessed one,
We celebrate the most glorious deeds you did
alone in the Lord,
 Ever-memorable Ephraim!//
Therefore we pray that you will intercede with
Christ for our souls!
(*Aposticha verses for the feast of St. Ephrem*)

As David wrote, you flourished like the palm tree,
Venerable Father Ephraim.
As with a sword, you cut off the tongues of
those who blasphemed.
With abstinence, you dried up the depths of the
passions.
You took up the Cross as a weapon

And were shown to be the instrument of the
Holy Spirit.
Ever pray to Christ on our behalf//
As we celebrate your honored memory with faith.
(*Matins Aposticha for feast of St. Ephrem*)

Ephrem was a prolific author, composing over
four hundred liturgical hymns as well as commentaries on entire books of Scripture. Below are a few of
the hymns that have been attributed to Ephrem. Take
note of the way that he uses scriptural imagery:

The assembly of saints
Bears resemblance to Paradise:
In it each day is plucked
The fruit of Him who gives life to all;
In it my brethren is trodden
The cluster of grapes, to be the Medicine of Life
The serpent is crippled and bound by the curse,
While Eve's mouth is sealed
With a silence that is beneficial
But it also serves once again
As a harp to sing the praises of her Creator
(Hymn 8 *Hymns on Paradise*)[2]

The lyre of the prophets who proclaimed Him,
singing before Him
And the hyssop of the priests who loved Him,
eagerly desiring his presence
And the diadem of kings who handed it down

---

[2] *St. Ephrem the Syrian Hymns on Paradise* trans. Translated
by Sebastian Brock (Crestwood, NY: St. Vladimir's Seminary
Press, 1990), p. 111.

in succession
Belong to this Lord of virgins, for even His
mother is a virgin.
He who is King gives the Kingdom to all.
He who is a Priest gives pardon to all.
He Who is the Lamb gives nourishment to all.
(Hymn 2 *Hymns on the Nativity*)[3]

Rely on the truth and fear not, my brothers,
For our Lord is not weak that He should desert
us in trials
He is the power on Whom depend the cre-
ation and its inhabitants
On Him depends the hope of His Church
Who is able to cut its heavenly roots?
Blessed is He Whose power came down and
was mingled with his churches!
Bestow on yourselves, my brothers, the trea-
sure of consolation
From the word our Lord spoke about His Church,
"The bars of Sheol cannot conquer her."
If indeed, she is mightier than Sheol,
Who among mortals can frighten her?
Blessed is He Who made her great yet has
tested her that she might be greater!
(*Hymns Against Julian; On The Church*)[4]

These examples are just a few of the hundreds of
hymns which Ephrem composed and are very rich
in biblical imagery.

---

[3] *Ephrem the Syrian Hymns.* Translated and introduction by
Kathleen E. McVey (Mahwah, NJ: Paulist Press, 1989), p. 76.
[4] Ibid, 221.

Ephrem wrote in Syriac, an ancient language related to Aramaic, the language which was spoken during the time of Jesus and the early Christians. Syriac is still used by members of the Jacobite Church of the East. His hymns were eventually translated into Greek, Latin and now into hundreds of languages. As a result of the large volume of hymns and poems, St. Ephrem has been called the Harp of the Sprit, the Pillar of the Church, and the Son of Syria. In iconography, St. Ephrem is usually portrayed in a monastic habit and portrayed as a scribe with paper and stylus in hand, sitting at his desk writing hymns. However, we are not sure whether or not Ephrem was really a monk. Monastic movements started throughout the Empire during the 4th century. People fled to remote areas, such as the deserts and the wilderness, to flee religious persecution and to fully commit themselves to living a solitary lifestyle based on prayer, fasting, and work. It is most likely that Ephrem lived within a community of single celibate Christians committing themselves fully to the Gospel. Much later they would be known as monastics. Likewise, it is doubtful that Ephrem would have worn a full monastic habit since habits were a much later addition to the monastic movement.

Today Ephrem is most widely known for the famous Lenten prayer which is used throughout Great Lent. It is highly likely that this prayer was written during the time of St. Ephrem, but we do not know for certain whether or not he actually composed the prayer. The prayer of St. Ephrem reflects the basic tenets of community life. Anyone who has lived in a family, college dormitory, parish or monastic community, knows full well the ups, downs, challenges and blessings of living together. It is not always easy! Ephrem draw on the tensions of communal life in the prayer:

> *O Lord and master of my life*
> *Take from me the spirit of sloth,*
> *despair, lust of power, and idle talk*
> *(prostration)*
> *But give rather the spirit of chastity,*
> *humility, patience, and love to Thy servant*
> *(prostration)*
> *Yes O Lord and king grant me to see my*
> *own sins*
> *And not to judge my brother*
> *For blessed art Thou unto the ages of*
> *ages amen.*
> *(prostration)*

This prayer is typically recited on the weekdays in Great Lent, especially during the celebration of the Liturgy of the Presanctified Gifts,[5] when it is recit-

---

[5] The Liturgy of the Presanctified Gifts is generally celebrated on Wednesday evenings during Great Lent. In some parishes, it is also celebrated on Friday evenings.

ed twice, and during other liturgical services, such as daily matins, vespers, and compline. This prayer can also be used in private devotion at home. Families can gather together in front of their icon corner and use this ancient prayer in their regular evening prayer routine. Even though this prayer is considered a Lenten prayer, it can be used throughout the year as a prayer of contrition, reflection and meditation. The words and phrases are food for thought as we struggle throughout the year.

The common practice is to recite each stanza and then make a full prostration to the ground. At the conclusion of the last stanza, we typically say in a quiet voice, "O Lord cleanse me a sinner and have mercy on me" twelve times, each time recited with a small prostration.[6] After the 12th "have mercy on me," the entire prayer is recited once again in full, followed by a single full prostration at the end. Some parish communities may follow a slightly different tradition, so the best advice is to follow the local custom.

In general, prostrations are foreign to people in the West. We are not prone to bowing to the ground. The act of prostrating oneself is humbling. No one likes getting down on their hands and knees. However, when we do prostrations, we are bowing down before God, who is our King, as an act of contrition and

---

[6] A full prostration means both head and hands on the floor (bowing down) while a small prostration is bending over and touching the ground.

humility, asking Him for forgiveness. We do prostrations in conjunction with the prayer of St. Ephrem so that our whole body becomes a prayer, both with our lips and with our body. In the ancient world, a vassal or servant would make prostrations before entering and exiting the king's chamber. Very often this "high court" etiquette is still performed today. Once I had the opportunity to participate in a Great Vespers service which was conducted by Patriarch Bartholomew, the Ecumenical Patriarch of Constantinople. Priests performed small prostrations before him as they asked for his blessing and then walked backwards to where they were previously standing so as to not turn their back towards him, which would be seen as an act of disrespect. My hunch is that this formal way of greeting the Patriarch was performed before the Emperor as an act of respect since in the ancient world, there was both an Emperor and a Patriarch.

The three prostrations together with the twelve shorter prostrations remind us of humility, our need of repentance, and that we often come up short when it comes to love, forgiveness, prayer, humility, and acts of charity. This prayer is used during Lent as a vehicle for introspection and to help us recognize our sins.

Reciting St. Ephrem's prayer with prostrations also reminds us that our whole body is praying. During worship, our whole body prays. We make the sign of the cross with our hands; we make prostrations when kissing icons at church; we cross our hands when we receive Holy Communion. We make processions around the church on Holy Friday, Easter night, and other times of the year.

The prayer of St. Ephrem is simple and firmly rooted in the Scriptures. When we take time to learn about the scriptural background and context of this prayer. Each stanza contains words like sloth, chastity, patience, and love; words that are formed in the Bible. The more we understand the biblical context of these words, the better we will understand the meaning of Great Lent.

This book can be used in personal devotional or used in conjunction with a small prayer group or adult Bible study. Take some time and read each chapter slowly, letting the words speak to you. Then make sure to read the Scripture selections that are included in each chapter. Likewise, at the conclusion of each chapter, you will find a section called "Food for Thought," which will help you better appreciate the themes of the chapter. These questions will help foster discussion and deeper reflection on the specific portion of the prayer. If you are in a small Bible study or prayer group, these questions can be used as a basis for your discussion. Some people may want to use these questions as a part of their spiritual journaling routine as well. Hopefully, these questions will lead to a good discussion about our discipleship and our common struggle with being faithful to the Gospel. The book also includes a bibliography for further reading about the life and writings of St. Ephrem as well as resources for the Lenten season.

Great Lent has often been called a "school for learning" since we once again learn and re-learn what it means to be faithful disciples of Jesus Christ, living, praying, and working in this world. The prayer is rich in meaning, and rooting it in the biblical text will provide you with a broader understanding of this gem of the Orthodox spiritual tradition. Hopefully, we can all learn to be faithful disciples of Jesus.

CHAPTER ONE

O LORD
AND MASTER

St. Ephrem's Prayer begins with a simple statement, "O Lord and Master of my life." We might not pay too much attention to the short opening, but it is a very important part of the prayer. The first stanza invites us to make a confession of faith: that God is the Lord and Master of our life. It is a confession very much like the beginning of the Nicene Creed, "I believe in one God," and in the short confession of faith that is used in the Orthodox Church right before receiving Holy Communion, "I believe O Lord and I confess that Thou art truly the Christ." These are two very public ways that we confess our faith in God.

This type of "confession" is also common among Jews and Muslims. Before praying, Jews always recite the Shema, "Hear O Israel the Lord our God is one Lord" (Deuteronomy 6:4), which according to Jewish custom must be recited twice per day. Likewise, Muslims, before opening the Koran, their holy book, recite the Shahada, "There is no God but Allah, and Mohammed is his prophet." The Shahada means "to testify," and it is one of the five spiritual pillars of Islam.[1]

The beginning of the prayer reminds us that we are not in control of life, a theme found in 12 step programs: Let go and let God. We are giving up control. Letting go is often extremely difficult because we are often tempted to control people, events, and situations. We want our lives to be perfect, having perfect houses, dressing up our children in the perfect clothes, being in the right clubs and groups. We spend so much time and effort trying to control situations, and we usually get upset in the process. Our plans to control people usually fail anyway.

This first petition is also a confirmation that God is ultimately in charge of the world and everything in it. He is our Judge and Creator; He is our Father and our source of life. We cannot say anything else before we first come before Him in humility and say, "O Lord and Master of my life."

This statement is even more important when we understand some of the biblical images connected with it. In the New Testament, terms like Lord and Master are attributed to Jesus. In Church, we often hear the phrase, "our Lord Jesus Christ," and usually do not give it a second thought. However, in the Roman Empire, especially in the lifetime of Jesus, the Emperor was called Lord and Master of the Universe.

---

[1] The other four pillars are Salat (praying five times a day), Zakat (alms-giving), Sawm (fasting), and Hajj (pilgrimage).

Augustus Caesar was the adopted son of Julius Caesar and was the Roman Emperor when Jesus was born. During Augustus' reign, emperor worship was commonplace and throughout the Empire. Every major city had a statue, a temple, or a shrine erected in his honor. Titles such as Lord, Master, and Savior were attributed to Augustus. He ruled the world and he made sure everyone knew it!

Therefore, when we learn more about the cultural and socio-political world of Jesus and the first Christians we realize the deeper meaning of these terms. Terms like Lord and Master were now attributed to Jesus and not the Emperor. St. Ephrem composed this prayer during the reign of Emperor Justinian in the eastern part of the Roman Empire. Justinian was an apostate, someone who rejected the Christian faith and this caused great upheaval in the Church. When people recited this prayer, they were also making a political statement, that they were putting their faith and trust in God the Father and not the Roman Emperor. This was also considered an act of disobedience, especially during times of religious persecution.

Before continuing, we acknowledge that we have no other help but God; no other gods or idols than the Lord and God and Savior Jesus Christ. He is our sole source of power and life. After we first acknowledge that God is our Lord and Master, then we can turn to the four major sins enumerated in the prayer: sloth, despair, lust of power, and idle talk.

SLOTH. One year when I was in elementary school, we were studying a unit on animals. I remember my teacher telling us about the different types of animals in the world. Each country was the home to special species of animals that were indigenous to that particular country. When we were learning about Central and South America, we learned about spiders, panthers, and pythons. We learned about the rain forest and the Amazon River. I also remember the teacher talking about sloths. I remember this because sloth is such a funny name. Sloths are small furry creatures that spend most of their time high up in the trees and do two things: eat and sleep. Their name fits them well. They are called sloths because they sleep for most of the day. Taking a nap is one thing, but spending all of your day napping is something else!

Having a spirit of sloth means that we are lazy. How often does your husband or wife ask you to take out the garbage or wash the dishes and you respond by saying, "I'll do it later dear," which roughly translates as, "I'll do it when I get off the couch or when it is convenient for me." In other words, you are being lazy or slothful!

Laziness comes in all shapes, forms, and sizes. I have met some people who do not want to do anything; if given the chance, they would sit at home and be couch potatoes! Sloth is not good. The Bible gives us several very colorful examples of the problem of laziness:

Go to the ant, O sluggard;
Consider her ways, and be wise.
Without having any chief,
Officer or ruler she prepares her food in summer, and gathers her sustenance in harvest.
How long will you lie there, O sluggard?
When will you arise from your sleep?
A little sleep, a little slumber and a little folding of The hands to rest,
And poverty will come upon you like a vagabond, and want like an armed man.
The way of a sluggard is overgrown with thorns, but the path of the upright is a level highway. (Proverbs 15:19)

"For it will be as when a man going on a journey called his servants and entrusted to them his property; to one he gave five talents, to another two, to another one, to each according to his ability. Then he went away. He who had received the five talents went at once and traded with them; and he made five talents more. So also, he who had the two talents made two talents more. But he who had received the one talent went and dug in the ground and hid his master's money. Now after a long time the master of those servants came and settled accounts with them. And he who had received the five talents came forward, bringing five talents more, saying, 'Master, you delivered to me five talents; here I have made five talents more.' Said to him, 'Well done, good and faithful servant; you have been faithful over a little, I will set you

over much; enter into the joy of your master.'
His master said to him, 'Well done, good and
faithful servant; you have been faithful over a
little, I will set you over much; enter into the
joy of your master.' He also who had received
the one talent came forward, saying, 'Master,
I knew you to be a hard man, reaping where
you did not sow, and gathering where you did
not winnow; so I was afraid, and I went and hid
your talent in the ground. Here you have what
is yours.' But his master answered him, 'You
wicked and slothful servant! You knew that I
reap where I have not sowed, and gather where
I have not winnowed? Then you ought to have
invested my money with the bankers, and at my
coming I should have received what was my
own with interest. So take the talent from him,
and give it to him who has the ten talents. For
to every one who has will more be given, and
he will have abundance; but from him who has
not, even what he has will be taken away. And
cast the worthless servant into the outer darkness; there men will weep and gnash their teeth'
(Matt. 25:14–30).

The first example is from the Book of Proverbs,
which is part of the Wisdom Literature. Proverbs is
a collection of wise pithy sayings or aphorisms that
have been collected and put together in one book. In
our culture, we have proverbs such as "a watched pot
never boils," "the faintest handwriting is better than
the best memory," or "measure twice, cut once." These

sayings are short, memorable, and passed down from generation to generation.

The example from Proverbs highlights the diligence and perseverance of the ant, which represents the worker. I usually see rows of marching ants moving back and forth across the lawn collecting food or pieces of bark or grass. Ants are no-nonsense creatures, traveling in straight lines carrying heavy burdens on their backs. The author of Proverbs tells us that the ant gathers food and, therefore, will have food during the harvest time. However, the slothful one or the sluggard is sleepy and lazy, letting life pass by without lifting a finger. The sluggard does not know how to work. He prefers to sit and watch someone else work. If ants do not work, they will not have food during the harvest time and will not be sustained. The proverb ends by saying that the way of the slothful person is overgrown with thorns, but the upright one, the one who is diligent and working, will have a level path, a clear way to walk. Surely we have met many people in life who are as diligent as the ant or as lazy as the sluggard.

This short example is followed by a much longer passage from the Gospel of Matthew. The king goes on a journey and leaves his servants at home and gives them each a talent, which is a type of currency. One servant gets five talents, the other two talents, and the last servant only one talent. The first two servants took their talents and multiplied them so the first one

had ten talents, the second one had four talents. The
last one did not invest the talent, he simply hid it and
returned it back upon his master's return. The problem is that the last servant was too scared or lazy or
lacking trust to invest the talent and did not create
more income for the master. And we hear at the end
of the lesson, "You wicked and slothful servant! You
knew that I reap where I have not sowed and gather
where I have not winnowed?" The servant was lazy
and did not work while the master was away. This
may be an extreme example, but it does hit home!
Many of the Lenten liturgical hymns also speak about
being slothful. We are called to be awake and vigilant
because we do not know the day or the hour of our
master's return. Below are only a few of the many examples taken from the first week of Lent:

> Soul, put aside the wicked sleep of laziness,
> And persevere with sincere vigilance in the
> Lord's commands.
> The torch-bearing Bridegroom is drawing near;
> Let us hasten to greet Him!
> Wounded by wicked pleasures,
> Heal me with the bountiful cure of Your mer-
> ciful divine will, O Word,
> And I will glorify You with thanksgiving forever.
>
> Restrain yourself, soul, from harmful passions,
> From hate and envy and from every evil.
> Be nourished in the Fast with the spiritual
> meat from heaven,
> Which is the Word of God.

(*Verses on Ode 2 Canon of Tuesday of the First Week of Lent*)

DESPAIR. Immediately after sloth we come across the word despair. Despair means the lack of faith or lack of hope. Having a spirit of despair means that you don't believe anymore. We have to fight against this because having a spirit of despair means that we do not trust God.

The opposite of despair is faith or trust. The Bible also uses the words steadfastness, endurance, or zeal as synonyms for faith. Having endurance means that we have to keep going forward, putting one foot in front of the other. We might want to think of a marathon. Running a marathon requires a lot of endurance to keep going. You pass the one, two, three, and five-mile markers, but you are not finished, you still have 17 miles to go! You cannot despair. You cannot look back at your past accomplishments. You have to keep going putting one foot in front of the other in order to finish the race. There are people who keep going forward no matter how hard the roadblocks may seem to be.

The words hope, faith, and trust, are rooted in the Scriptures. The authors of the various books of the Bible encourage people to put their faith and trust in God. Trusting people will only lead to despair, as we hear in the Beatitudes, "Do not put your trust in princess in whom there is no salvation." When we put our trust in politicians, athletes, rock stars, media moguls, the rich and the wealthy, we will always be discouraged. Other people will eventually fail us. The problem is that we put famous people on pedestals. We forget that they are just as frail and broken as we are. However, the Lord never fails; as the Psalms tell us, He is our rock and our fortress.

The Apostle Paul put his trust in the Lord. Paul endured many hardships and troubles in life: shipwrecked, beaten with rods, put into prison, and thrown out of town. Yet despite Paul's difficult life, he still had hope. His letters are full of words like hope, faith, or trust, and very often a combination of all three:

> Therefore, since we are justified by faith, we have peace with God through our Lord Jesus Christ. Through him we have obtained access to this grace in which we stand, and we rejoice in our hope of sharing the glory of God. More than that, we rejoice in our sufferings, knowing that suffering produces endurance, and endurance produces character, and character produces hope, and hope does not disappoint us, because God's love has been poured into our hearts through the Holy Spirit which has been given to us. While we were still weak, at the right time Christ died for the ungodly. Why, one will hardly die for a righteous man — though perhaps for a good man one will dare even to die. But God shows his love for us in that while we were yet sinners Christ died for us. Since, therefore, we are now justified by his blood, much more shall we be saved by him from the

wrath of God. For if while we were enemies we were reconciled to God by the death of his Son, much more, now that we are reconciled, shall we be saved by his life. Not only so, but we also rejoice in God through our Lord Jesus Christ, through whom we have now received our reconciliation (Romans 5:1–11).

Grace to you and peace from God the Father and the Lord Jesus Christ. We are bound to give thanks to God always for you, brethren, as is fitting, because your faith is growing abundantly, and the love of every one of you for one another is increasing. We ourselves boast of you in the churches of God for your steadfastness and faith in all your persecutions and in the afflictions which you are enduring. This is evidence of the righteous judgment of God, that you may be made worthy of the kingdom of God, for which you are suffering — since indeed God deems it just to repay with affliction those who afflict you, and to grant rest with us to you who are afflicted, when the Lord Jesus is revealed from heaven with his mighty angels in flaming fire, inflicting vengeance upon those who do not know God and upon those who do not obey the gospel of our Lord Jesus. They shall suffer the punishment of eternal destruction and exclusion from the presence of the Lord and from the glory of his might, when he comes on that day to be glorified in his saints, and to be marveled at in all who have believed, because our testimony to you was believed (2 Thess. 1:2–11).

In the first example from Romans, Paul wants to encourage his community to be faithful even in times of persecution and difficulty. We have to remember that Paul was writing to the Christian community in Rome which was most likely a small community. The Roman Christians were a minority among the other Roman citizens who were pagan Gentiles or Jews. Rome was the capital of the Empire and, in terms of the Roman mind, it was also considered the center of the world. The Christians in Rome would have to deal with the Emperor, the Senate, the military, and the heart of the Roman economy. Paul was fully aware of the Roman culture and encouraged the Roman Church to maintain their faith in Jesus, not in Caesar, Apollo, or Zeus. We can see the progression of Paul's message below:

Suffering = Endurance
Endurance= Character
Character = Hope

Paul reminds his readers that their afflictions will eventually produce hope if they maintain their trust in the Lord. This same sentiment is also highlighted in his second letter to the Thessalonians, where he says, "Because your faith is growing abundantly, and the love of every one of you for one another is increasing, we ourselves boast of you in the churches of God for your steadfastness and faith in all your persecutions and in their afflictions which you are enduring."

Then, of course, we come to a familiar passage from the book of Hebrews. In the Orthodox Church, this particular passage is read on the Sunday before Christmas and reminds us of all the people who lived prior to Jesus and yet never saw the birth of the Messiah:

> Now faith is the assurance of things hoped for, the conviction of things not seen. For by it the men of old received divine approval. By faith we understand that the world was created by the word of God, so that what is seen was made out of things which do not appear. By faith Abel offered to God a more acceptable sacrifice than Cain, through which he received approval as righteous, God bearing witness by accepting his gifts; he died, but through his faith he is still speaking. By faith Enoch was taken up so that he should not see death; and he was not found, because God had taken him. Now before he was taken he was attested as having pleased God. And without faith it is impossible to please him. For whoever would draw near to God must believe that he exists and that he rewards those who seek him. By faith Noah, being warned by God concerning events as yet unseen, took heed and constructed an ark for the saving of his household; by this he condemned the world and became an heir of the righteousness which comes by faith (Hebrews 11:1–7).

We are reminded that God was working in people a long time before Jesus was born. In this passage we hear about Abel, Noah, and Enoch, but when

reading further we see that the author also includes
Abraham, Isaac, Jacob, Essau, Moses, Gideon, Sam-
son, Barak, David, and Samuel; people enumerated
in this long list of names were called to follow God.
They walked the life of faith even though they could
not see the fruits of their labors. Moses for example
was called to lead the Israelites out of Egypt which
he did but he died before they entered the promised
land. It was Moses' young helper, Joshua, the son of
Nun, who buried Moses and then lead Israel into Ca-
naan. Likewise Abraham was granted the blessing
to be the father of all nations. Abraham's trust in the
Lord resulted in the birth of Isaac who was the son
of the promise. The book of Hebrews says that their
lives were not easy; "others suffered mocking and
scourging, and even chains and imprisonment. They
were stoned, they were sawn in two, they were killed
with the sword; they went about in skins of sheep
and goats, destitute, afflicted, ill treated- of whom the
world was not worthy-wandering over deserts and
mountains, and in dens and caves of the earth" (Hebrews 11:36–38).

L UST OF POWER. The third sin mentioned in the
prayer is lust of power. Anyone following the
news about the Wall Street scandals knows full well
the lure of power and control. One corporate executive redecorated his office with lavish sideboards
and imported rugs totaling over $75,000! After all

was said and done, he made a public apology, saying that he should have shopped at IKEA instead. People laughed at this remark, but at the root of all of that is a major problem with power. The executive did not realize that he was spending good company money, money which investors had entrusted for investment and corporate improvement, which was squandered on rugs, desks, and office supplies. Power, if left unchecked, often results in the wasting of money.

Lord Acton, a powerful British leader, once said, "Power tends to corrupt, and absolute power corrupts absolutely." Power in the hands of a few usually leads to corruption and scandal. One of the benefits of living in the United States is our three branches of government are separated. Major decisions in our country, especially involving legal issues and making new laws, have to go through the Senate, the House of Representatives, as well as the President. No one branch of government controls life in our country.

The Bible includes many examples of people who abused their power. One glaring example is Judas, one of Jesus' closest friends and disciples. Judas was in charge of the treasury. As Jesus and His disciples went throughout the Galilee area preaching the Gospel, people would have given Jesus donations for His ministry. As the treasurer, Judas was responsible for those funds. The Pharisees came to Judas asking him to betray Jesus, and he agreed to do it for thirty pieces of silver. Thirty pieces of silver may not seem like a lot of money today, but during the time of Jesus, it was a lot of money. We can see how the temptation of money and of power corrupts people. The liturgical hymns for Holy Wednesday speak about Judas and his sinful actions as a reminder to us, that temptation for power is there all the time:

> Today Judas abandons all pretense of love for the poor.
> Not caring for them, he assumes the very shape of greed.
> Instead of selling the sinful woman's myrrh,
> He sells the Anointed One of God and steals the proceeds.
> He runs to the lawless Jews and asks:
> What will you give me if I betray Him to you?
> Cursed be the traitor's love of silver!
> He lowers the price and bargains like a trader.
> He sells Jesus like a runaway slave, not asking much.
> For thieves never regard the value of precious things;
> Now the disciple casts holy things to the dogs.
> Maddened with avarice, he howls against the Master.
> Let us flee from his example and cry://
> Long-suffering Lord, glory to You!
> (*Aposticha Matins of Holy Friday*)

The Gospels show us other examples of power. Jesus was born during the reign of King Herod the Great, the King of Judea. Herod was a client king who was working for the Roman government. He was Jewish by birth but was sent by the Roman government to serve as their local king. Herod owed his allegiance to the Roman Emperor despite the fact that he was part Jewish. He oversaw numerous building projects during his lifetime: Caesarea Philipi, Caesarea Marit-mima, as well as one of his vacation homes near Bethlehem. He was extremely wealthy and powerful. Yet when Herod heard from the Magi the news of Jesus' birth, he went crazy, "Then Herod when he saw that he had been tricked by the wise men, was in a furious rage, and he sent and killed all the male children in Bethlehem and in all that region who were two years old or under, according to the time which he had ascertained from the wise men" (Matthew 2:16). So Herod went out and, as Matthew says, went on a rampage and murdered the children who were two years old or younger. Herod and Jesus are two good examples of the damage done when people give into the temptation of power and control.

IDLE TALK. Finally, we come to the fourth major sin mentioned in the prayer, which is the sin of idle talk. Idle talk is also referred to as gossip or using empty words. A lot of people have trouble with idle talk. The workplace tends to be a major temptation for people. You might see a co-worker in the hall or during lunchtime, and all of a sudden, they begin talking about a fellow co-worker. They point out personality traits or other problems with the person. After a while, the conversation snow-balls, and they start talking about other people. People quickly offer opinions.

The internet is a wonderful vehicle for communication, but even the internet can be a temptation for idle talk and gossip. New social media sites, like Twitter, Facebook, and Myspace, can lead to gossip. Sometimes, the consequences are deadly. A new term called "cyber-bullying" is used for people who spread lies, gossip, or who try to defame people. Teenagers will get on these social network sites and spread rumors friends or other classmates at school, sometimes including pictures, and there is no stopping once it goes onto the internet. Once you post something, it is there for a long time. Not only do peoples' feelings get hurt, but sometimes the victims have low self esteem or suicidal thoughts. Cyber bullying is a technologically new way of gossip, but it is gossip nonetheless.

Below are several examples from the Scriptures and the liturgical hymns that speak about about idle talk:

> Death and life are in the power of the tongue, and those who love it will eat its fruits. (Proverbs 18:21)

> With his mouth the godless man would destroy his neighbor, but by knowledge the righteous are delivered. (Proverbs 11:9)

> The words of the wicked lie in wait for blood, but the mouth of the upright delivers men. (Proverbs 12:6)

An evil man is ensnared by the transgression of his lips, but the righteous escapes from trouble. From the fruit of his words a man is satisfied with good, and the work of a man's hand comes back to him. (Proverbs 12:13–14)

Either make the tree good, and its fruit good; or make the tree bad, and its fruit bad; for the tree is known by its fruit. You brood of vipers! how can you speak good, when you are evil? For out of the abundance of the heart the mouth speaks. The good man out of his good treasure brings forth good, and the evil man out of his evil treasure brings forth evil. I tell you, on the day of judgment men will render account for every careless word they utter; for by your words you will be justified, and by your words you will be condemned." (Matthew 12:33–37)

And the tongue is a fire. The tongue is an unrighteous world among our members, staining the whole body, setting on fire the cycle of nature, and set on fire by hell. For every kind of beast and bird, of reptile and sea creature, can be tamed and has been tamed by humankind, but no human being can tame the tongue — a restless evil, full of deadly poison. With it we bless the Lord and Father, and with it we curse men, who are made in the likeness of God. From the same mouth come blessing and cursing. My brethren, this ought not to be so. Does a spring pour forth from the same opening fresh water and brackish? Can a fig tree, my brethren, yield olives, or a grapevine figs? No more can salt water yield fresh (James 3:6–12).

The first few examples from Proverbs speak about the problems of idle talk; it is destructive, is the opposite of knowledge, and brings down. The examples from the New Testament, primarily from James and Matthew, take up these examples from Proverbs and expand upon them. James begins his passage in the following way, "And the tongue is a fire. The tongue is an unrighteous world among our members, staining the whole body, setting on fire the cycle of nature, and set on fire by hell." What an image; the tongue as fire! A fire devours and burns everything up. James warns people in his community to refrain from idle talking since it leads to destruction and major divisions. Matthew too takes this up in his Gospel as Jesus tells us that we will be judged for every false word that we say. It is important to be careful of not only what we say but how we say it. These few examples give us a lifetime of wisdom as we go about our daily activities interacting with other people in a humane way and trying not to talk about them behind their backs.

Food For Thought

1. Take some time and reflect on the times that you have been lazy. Are you lazy once in a while or is it a habitual problem?

2. Identify times that you felt hopeless? What was the situation? How did you overcome these feelings?

3. Power effects people differently. Some people in positions of power feel a deep humility knowing that they have power over people. Others are oblivious to their power and use it without thinking of other people's feelings. Do you have power over anyone in life — at work? At home? In your parish? How do you exercise power?

4. Do find yourself gossiping about other people? If so, try to identify some ways in which you refrain from gossip and idle talk.

CHAPTER TWO

BUT RATHER
GIVE ME

While the first portion of St. Ephrem's prayer lays out the common sins of the spiritual life, the second stanza provides us with four positive qualities or virtues of the Christian life. Here we are asking God for chastity, humility, patience, and love. Each of these virtues counterbalances the four sins mentioned above. Each of the four virtues are to be fostered, encouraged, and cultivated during Lent and throughout the rest of our life.

CHASTITY. Chastity is not a common word in our vocabulary. Chastity means having good intentions, having a spirit of innocence and purity, and being upright. It means that we try to have a pure heart, seeking the good in all things. The opposite of chastity is self-righteousness, greed, pride, and selfishness. Chastity also means being pure sexually.

Being chaste is not easy. If we hear that a co-worker did well on their job and received a raise, we may

say, "Well, that's nice, but I received a raise last year."
We downplay someone else's good news by immediately focusing on our accomplishments. The Beatitudes from Matthew's Gospel teach us that when we
are chaste, we will be able to see God, "Blessed are the
pure in heart for they shall see God" (Matthew 5:8).

The book of Psalms contain many examples of
purity of heart. Below are just three examples that
show us how the Psalms explain the nature of purity:

> The earth is the Lord's and the fullness thereof,
> The world and those who dwell therein;
> For he has founded it upon the seas,
> And established it upon the rivers. Who shall
> ascend the hill of the Lord?
> And who shall stand in his holy place?
> He who has clean hands and a pure heart,
> Who does not lift up his soul to what is false,
> And does not swear deceitfully.
> He will receive blessing from the Lord,
> And vindication from the God of his salvation.
> Such is the generation of those who seek him,
> Who seek the face of the God of Jacob. [Selah]
> Lift up your heads, O gates!
> And be lifted up, O ancient doors!
> That the King of glory may come in.
> Who is the King of glory?
> The Lord, strong and mighty,
> The Lord, mighty in battle!
> Lift up your heads, O gates!
> And be lifted up, O ancient doors!
> That the King of glory may come in.

Who is this King of glory?
The Lord of hosts,
He is the King of glory!
(Psalm 24)

Have mercy on me, O God,
According to thy steadfast love;
According to thy abundant mercy blot out my
transgressions.
Wash me thoroughly from my iniquity,
And cleanse me from my sin!
For I know my transgressions,
And my sin is ever before me.
Against thee, thee only, have I sinned,
And done that which is evil in thy sight,
So that thou art justified in thy sentence
And blameless in thy judgment.
Behold, I was brought forth in iniquity,
And in sin did my mother conceive me.
Behold, thou desirest truth in the inward being;
Therefore teach me wisdom in my secret heart.
Purge me with hyssop, and I shall be clean;
Wash me, and I shall be whiter than snow.
Fill me with joy and gladness;
Let the bones which thou hast broken rejoice.
Hide thy face from my sins,
And blot out all my iniquities.
Create in me a clean heart, O God,
And put a new and right spirit within me.
Cast me not away from thy presence,
And take not thy holy Spirit from me.
Restore to me the joy of thy salvation,
And uphold me with a willing spirit.

Then I will teach transgressors thy ways,
And sinners will return to thee.
Deliver me from bloodguiltiness, O God,
Thou God of my salvation,
And my tongue will sing aloud of thy deliverance.
O Lord, open thou my lips,
And my mouth shall show forth thy praise.
For thou hast no delight in sacrifice;
Were I to give a burnt offering, thou wouldst
not be pleased.
The sacrifice acceptable to God is a broken spirit;
A broken and contrite heart, O God, thou wilt
not despise.
Do good to Zion in thy good pleasure;
Rebuild the walls of Jerusalem,
Then wilt thou delight in right sacrifices,
In burnt offerings and whole burnt offerings;
Then bulls will be offered on thy altar.
(Psalm 51)

Truly God is good to the upright,
To those who are pure in heart.
But as for me, my feet had almost stumbled,
My steps had well nigh slipped.
For I was envious of the arrogant,
When I saw the prosperity of the wicked.
For they have no pangs;
Their bodies are sound and sleek.
They are not in trouble as other men are;
They are not stricken like other men.
Therefore pride is their necklace;
Violence covers them as a garment.
Their eyes swell out with fatness,

Their hearts overflow with follies.
They scoff and speak with malice;
Loftily they threaten oppression.
They set their mouths against the heavens,
And their tongue struts through the earth.
Therefore the people turn and praise them;
And find no fault in them.
(Psalm 73:1–10)

Probably the best known example from the selections above is Psalm 51, which tradition states was written by David after he fell into an adulterous affair with Bathsheba. David had Bathsheba's husband Uzziah sent into battle knowing full well that Uzziah's troops would probably loose. Not only did they lose, but Uzziah was killed during the battle. This allowed David to take Bathsheba as his lover. This Psalm is one of repentance and forgiveness of sins, asking God to purify David's heart again since he sinned in a grave manner.

The Gospels also speak of chastity and purity. Towards the end of Jesus' life, as He was eating the Passover meal with His disciples, an unnamed woman, whose identity is sometimes conflated with that of a "sinful woman" mentioned in the Gospel of Luke, washes Jesus' feet with her hair. John mentions that her name was Mary, the sister of Martha, who were both sisters of Lazarus, whom Jesus raised from the dead (John 11). This reading, as well as the liturgical hymns attributed to her, are powerful images to reflect upon during the Lenten journey:

Six days before the Passover, Jesus came to Bethany, where Lazarus was, whom Jesus had raised from the dead. There they made him a supper; Martha served, and Lazarus was one of those at table with him. Mary took a pound of costly ointment of pure nard and anointed the feet of Jesus and wiped his feet with her hair; and the house was filled with the fragrance of the ointment. But Judas Iscariot, one of his disciples (he who was to betray him), said, "Why was this ointment not sold for three hundred denarii and given to the poor?" This he said, not that he cared for the poor but because he was a thief, and as he had the money box he used to take what was put into it. Jesus said, "Let her alone, let her keep it for the day of my burial. The poor you always have with you, but you do not always have me." (John 12:1–8)

In tears the harlot cried out, compassionate one,
As she fervently wiped your most pure feet with the hair of her head,
And she groaned from the depths of her soul:
Cast me not away, neither abhor me, my God,
But receive me in my repentance and save me,//
For You alone are the lover of mankind.
A harlot recognized You as God, O Son of the Virgin.
With tears equal to her past deeds, she besought you weeping:
Loose my debt as I have loosed my hair.
Love the woman who, though justly hated, loves you.

Then with the Publicans will I proclaim you,//
Benefactor and lover of mankind.

The harlot mingled precious myrrh with her tears.
She poured it on Your most pure feet and kissed
them.
At once you justified her.
You suffered for our sakes://
Forgive us also, and save us.

As the sinful woman was bringing her offering
of myrrh,
The disciple was scheming with lawless men.
She rejoiced in pouring out her precious gift.
He hastened to sell the precious one.
She recognized the Master, but Judas parted
from Him.
She was set free, but Judas was enslaved to the
enemy.
How terrible is slothfulness!
How great her repentance!
Savior, You suffered for our sakes://
Grant us also repentance, and save us.
(*Praises Bridegroom Matins Holy Wednesday*)

We do not know whether or not this woman was
a prostitute or not; however, washing Jesus' feet with
her hair was a noble task. It was not beneath her to
wash His feet, an act of humility and contrition. John
also mentions that Jesus Himself washed the feet of
His disciples as well, the act of serving the brother
and the sister is a priority with Jesus. This woman's
action is pure and innocent, a real act of chastity.

HUMILITY. If we think chastity is difficult, perhaps humility is even more difficult!

Being humble means that you put yourself second, third, or even fourth. Being humble means that we do not boast about ourselves or have bad intentions for other people. The word humility is derived from the Latin word humus, the dark rich organic material used in gardening. We also refer to humus as compost.

Compost is that rich dark earthy material that we add to our garden soil. When we till compost into the ground, it releases all of its nutrients and minerals and feeds the seeds and plants. Compost is usually full of worms and bugs. We have a compost pile in the backyard and everything from our kitchen goes into the compost pile: banana peels, apple cores, coffee grinds, eggshells, cucumber peelings, rotten tomatoes, and so forth. This organic material is put into a big garbage container and sits. With sun and some moisture, the compost begins to rot and decompose. Once in a while, I open the cover and see worms and bugs feeding off the rotting food. The compost pile also smells very bad. When the food begins to decompose, it is ready to be worked into the ground. This is the best material for gardening, sometimes it is called "black gold" because of the large quantity of vitamins and minerals contained in it.

Being humble means that the egotistical and selfish part of us has to die. Our pride, anger, envy, and agendas need to be broken down so that we can give more and more into love. Our rough edges are made soft and smooth like river rocks in a stream. At one time, river rocks were rough, craggy and very ugly. At one time, that rock had nooks and crannies and plenty of dirt on it. Yet, over time with the rushing water running over it, the roughness has been worked out and now you see the gentle surface of the rock. The river rock is like our life. When we are humble and serve other people, the rough edges and dirt within us are washed away and made smooth. Our Christian faith reminds us that we are to put the needs of the neighbor first, as we see in the following Scripture passage:

> He has showed you, O man, what is good;
> And what does the Lord require of you
> But to do justice, and to love kindness,
> And to walk humbly with your God?
> (Micah 6:8)

> At that time the disciples came to Jesus, saying, "Who is the greatest in the kingdom of heaven?" And calling to him a child, he put him in the midst of them, and said, "Truly, I say to you, unless you turn and become like children, you will never enter the kingdom of heaven. Whoever humbles himself like this child, he is the greatest in the kingdom of heaven. "Whoever receives one such child in my name receives me; but whoever causes one of these little ones to believe in me to sin; it would be better for

him to have a great millstone fastened around his neck to be drowned in the depth of the sea. (Matthew 18:1–5)

Then said Jesus to the crowds and to his disciples, "The scribes and the Pharisees sit on Moses' seat; so practice and observe whatever they tell you, but not what they do; for they preach, but do not practice. They bind heavy burdens, hard to bear, and lay them on men's shoulders; but they themselves will not move them with their finger. They do all their deeds to be seen by men; for they make their phylacteries broad and their fringes long, and they love the place of honor at feasts and the best seats in the synagogues, and salutations in the market places, and being called rabbi by men. But you are not to be called rabbi, for you have one teacher, and you are all brethren. And call no man your father on earth, for you have one Father, who is in heaven. Neither be called masters, for you have one master, the Christ. He who is greatest among you shall be your servant; whoever exalts himself will be humbled, and whoever humbles himself will be exalted.
(Matthew 23:1–12)

So I exhort the elders among you, as a fellow elder and a witness of the sufferings of Christ as well as a partaker in the glory that is to be revealed. Tend the flock of God that is your charge, not by constraint but willingly, not for shameful gain but eagerly, not as domineering over those in your charge but being examples to the flock.

And when the chief Shepherd is manifested you will obtain the unfading crown of glory. Likewise you that are younger be subject to the elders. Clothe yourselves, all of you, with humility toward one another, for "God opposes the proud, but gives grace to the humble." Humble yourselves therefore under the mighty hand of God, that in due time he may exalt you. Cast all your anxieties on him, for he cares about you. Be sober, be watchful. Your adversary the devil prowls around like a roaring lion, seeking some one to devour. Resist him, firm in your faith, knowing that the same experience of suffering is required of your brotherhood throughout the world. And after you have suffered a little while, the God of all grace, who has called you to his eternal glory in Christ, will himself restore, establish, and strengthen you. To him be the dominion for ever and ever. Amen.
(1 Peter 5:1–11)

There are plenty of other examples of humility in the Scriptures. Needless to say, these examples show us that humility is important. Matthew gives us the example of a child who is totally dependent on their parents for help; children need clothing, food, shelter, and protection, otherwise they will certainly die. A child is innocent in the eyes of the world. A child is helpless and dependent on other people. They are dependent on their parents for everything in life.

The last example is from the Gospel of Matthew which is read during Bridegroom Matins during Holy

Week. The teachings are near the end of the Gospel as Jesus is going to His betrayal, trial, and the cross. He warns His disciples about the pride and arrogance of the Pharisees who sit on Moses' seat and preach but do not practice. This is a warning to His disciples that if they are to be great, they are to serve others, not lord it over them as do the Jewish leaders. We know that Jesus gave us a great example of humility as He washed the feet of His disciples. He stooped down, took off His clothes and began to wash the disciples' feet. In the Church, we commemorate this event at the Divine Liturgy on Holy Thursday:

> Now before the feast of the Passover, when Jesus knew that His hour had come to depart out of this world to the Father, having loved His own who were in the world, He loved them to the end. And during supper, when the devil had already put it into the heart of Judas Iscariot, Simon's son, to betray Him, Jesus, knowing that the Father had given all things into His hands, and that He had come from God and was going to God, rose from supper, laid aside His garments, and girded Himself with a towel. Then He poured water into a basin, and began to wash the disciples' feet, and to wipe them with the towel with which He was girded. He came to Simon Peter; and Peter said to Him, "Lord, do you wash my feet?" Jesus answered him, "What I am doing you do not know now, but afterward you will understand." Peter said to Him, "You shall never wash my feet." Jesus

answered him, "If I do not wash you, you have no part in Me." Simon Peter said to Him, "Lord, not my feet only but also my hands and my head!" Jesus said to him, "He who has bathed does not need to wash, except for his feet, but he is clean all over; and you are clean, but not every one of you." For He knew who was to betray Him; that was why He said, "You are not all clean." When He had washed their feet, and taken His garments, and resumed His place, He said to them, "Do you know what I have done to you? You call Me Teacher and Lord; and you are right, for so I am. If I then, your Lord and Teacher, have washed your feet, you also ought to wash one another's feet. For I have given you an example, that you also should do as I have done to you. Truly, truly, I say to you, a servant is not greater than his master; nor is he who is sent greater than he who sent him. If you know these things, blessed are you if you do them.

Jesus concludes this saying by inviting Peter and the other disciples to wash one another's feet as well. This is not an option. Service and discipleship are closely linked. We are called to follow Christ who gave us multiple examples of serving others. Washing feet is a dirty and menial task. During the time of Jesus, there were slaves who were assigned to wash the feet of guests who would come to visit them. However, Jesus stoops down like a slave and washes feet. Hopefully, the image of Jesus washing feet will be an image of humility and service:

In Your goodness You humbled Yourself,
Washing the feet of your disciples.
Peter would not allow this, not seeing the divine plan.
When You revealed it, he obeyed and was washed!//
We fervently pray to You: Grant unto us great mercy!
(*Ode 1 Canon Matins of Holy Friday*)

Instructing Your disciples in the mystery, Lord,
You said to them:
My beloved, see that no fear separates you from me.
Though I suffer, it is for the sake of the world.
Let Me not be a cause of scandal to you.
I came, not to be served, but to serve,
To give myself for the redemption of the world.
If you are My friends, then imitate me.
Let the first among you be the last.
Let the master be like the servant.//
Abide in me and bear fruit, for I am the Vine of Life.
(*Aposticha Matins for Holy Friday*)

Brothers, let us not pray like the Pharisee:
He who exalts himself will be humbled!
Let us prepare to abase ourselves by fasting;
Let us cry aloud with the voice of the Publican://
O God, forgive us sinners!

The Pharisee went up to the temple with a proud and empty heart;
The Publican bowed himself in repentance.
They both stood before You, O Master:
The one, through boasting, lost his reward,

But the other, with tears and sighs, won Your
blessing:
Strengthen me, O Christ our God, as I weep in
Your presence,//
Since You are the lover of mankind!
(*Lord I Call Publican and the Pharisee*)

PATIENCE. Then we come to the next word in the
prayer — patience. Patience and humility go together. When we seek humility, we also seek patience.
We might be familiar with the phrase "having the patience of Job" a common cultural phrase that comes
right out of the Old Testament. Job is the epitome of
suffering. The book of Job is very long and you are encouraged to read it on your own. Take time because
there is a lot to digest in that short book. The book
begins on a good note. Job is doing well in life. He
has a farm with lands and animals. He has a beauti-
ful wife and children. However, all of a sudden Satan
comes to God inquiring whether or not God's creatures are strong.[1] God responds to Satan by saying
that he may do anything to Job except take his life.
God allows Satan to tempt Job.

Slowly Job's life is stripped away. A famine comes
and all the animals die. Then invaders come and take
Job's daughters. His sons are killed in battle. Job is then
afflicted with terrible sores over his body. His life is in

---

[1] The name Satan means "the deceiver" and is also referred to
as the devil or Lucifer in the Christian tradition.

shambles. His wife finally tells Job to curse God and die, and then she abandons him. Even his friends come and tell him that he is crazy. Yet Job never rejects God. Job's suffering reminds him of his faith in the Lord:

> And the Lord restored the fortunes of Job, when he had prayed for his friends; and the Lord gave Job twice as much as he had before. Then came to him all his brothers and sisters and all who had known him before, and ate bread with him in his house; and they showed him sympathy and comforted him for all the evil that the Lord had brought upon him; and each of them gave him a piece of money and a ring of gold. And the Lord blessed the latter days of Job more than his beginning; and he had fourteen thousand sheep, six thousand camels, a thousand yoke of oxen, and a thousand she-asses. He had also seven sons and three daughters. And he called the name of the first Jemimiah; and the name of the second Kezi'ah; and the name of the third Ker'en-hap'puch. And in all the land there were no women so fair as Job's daughters; and their father gave them inheritance among their brothers. And after this Job lived a hundred and forty years, and saw his sons, and his sons' sons, four generations. And Job died, an old man, and full of days (Job 42:10–17).

> Therefore, since we are surrounded by so great a cloud of witnesses, let us also lay aside every weight, and sin which clings so closely, and let us run with perseverance the race that is set before us, looking to Jesus the pioneer and per-

fecter of our faith, who for the joy that was set before Him endured the cross, despising the shame, and is seated at the right hand of the throne of God (Hebrews 12:1–2).

Therefore, since we are justified by faith, we have peace with God through our Lord Jesus Christ. Through Him we have obtained access to this grace in which we stand, and we rejoice in our hope of sharing the glory of God. More than that, we rejoice in our sufferings, knowing that suffering produces endurance, and endurance produces character, and character produces hope, and hope does not disappoint us, because God's love has been poured into our hearts through the Holy Spirit which has been given to us (Romans 5:1–5).

As He sat on the Mount of Olives, the disciples came to Him privately, saying, "Tell us, when will this be, and what will be the sign of your coming and of the close of the age?" And Jesus answered them, "Take heed that no one leads you astray. For many will come in My name, saying, 'I am the Christ,' and they will lead many astray. And you will hear of wars and rumors of wars; see that you are not alarmed; for this must take place, but the end is not yet. For nation will rise against nation, and kingdom against kingdom, and there will be famines and earthquakes in various places: all this is but the beginning of the birth-pangs. "Then they will deliver you up to tribulation, and put you to death; and you will be hated by all nations for my name's sake.

And then many will fall away, and betray one
another, and hate one another. And many false
prophets will arise and lead many astray. And
because wickedness is multiplied, most men's
love will grow cold. But he who endures to the
end will be saved. And this Gospel of the kingdom will be preached throughout the whole
world, as a testimony to all nations; and then
the end will come (Matthew 24:3–14).

All of these examples speak to patience and the
spiritual life. Patience is also connected to endurance
and perseverance, especially in light of hardships and
suffering. So much of our life is waiting. When we
go to the doctor's office for a medical exam, we often have to wait for the results. High school children
must wait to hear about their college acceptance letters. Parents have to wait nine months for a baby to
be born. Most of our life is spent waiting for something or someone! Waiting can be difficult.

Yet patience requires resilience and fortitude. We
have to keep in mind that the early Christians lived in
a world different than our own. They were a minority in a world with many gods and idols. Christians
were often persecuted for their faith in Jesus. We
have many stories of early Christian martyrs such as
Perpetua and Felicitas, St. Ignatius of Antioch, Poly-
carp of Smyrna, as well as Irenaeus of Lyons.[1] These

---

[1] For more information about the early martyrs, see the stories of
Perpetua and Felicitas, Irenaeus of Lyons, and Ignatius of Antioch.

authors wrote to their communities during times of great persecutions, arrests, trials, and public displays of death.

Patience requires endurance, that we will put one foot in front of the other keeping our faith steady and strong. We cannot waiver in light of suffering. Many stories of martyred saints are read as a source of inspiration for people.

L OVE. The last virtue in this portion of the prayer is love. The word "love" is used very loosely in our culture. People often say that they love their new car just the same as they love their new home. When we say that we love our new car, we really mean that we really like that car. Or when we say that we love our new sports jacket because it matches the new home, it means that we really enjoy it. On St. Valentine's Day, we exchange chocolates and greeting cards as signs of our love. We give gifts at birthdays, anniversaries, and at Christmas time as a sign of love.

According to the New Testament, love is always connected with the cross. The cross is where God shows His perfect love for us, "for God so loved the world that He gave His only begotten so that we should not perish but have everlasting life." The cross is an image of sacrifice. Jesus went to Golgotha because He loved the world and everything in the world. In reality, the cross is Jesus' final word to us. His entire ministry was based on love. He went to the lepers and the outcasts because He loved them and wanted them to be reconciled to the community. He spent time with harlots and prostitutes because He loved them and wanted them to change their ways. He loved His disciples, even though they often rejected His teachings and doubted His power. Towards the end of His life, Jesus taught His disciples, "A new commandment I give to you, that you love one another; even as I have loved you, that you also love one another. By this all men will know that you are My disciples, if you have love for one another."

> If you love Me, you will keep My commandments. And I will pray the Father, and He will give you another Counselor, to be with you for ever, even the Spirit of truth, whom the world cannot receive, because it neither sees Him nor knows Him; you know Him, for He dwells with you, and will be in you. "I will not leave you desolate; I will come to you. Yet a little while, and the world will see Me no more, but you will see Me; because I live, you will live also. In that day you will know that I am in My Father, and you in Me, and I in you. He who has my commandments and keeps them, he it is who loves Me; and he who loves Me will be loved by My Father, and I will love him and manifest Myself to him." Judas (not Iscariot) said to Him, "Lord, how is it that You will manifest Yourself to us, and not to the world?" Jesus answered him, "If a man loves Me, he will keep My word, and My Father will love him, and We will come to him

and make Our home with him. He who does not love Me does not keep My words; and the word which you hear is not Mine but the Father's who sent Me.

Jesus also taught us to love God with all our heart, soul, mind and strength, "You shall love the Lord your God with all your heart, and with all your soul, and with all your mind. This is the great and first commandment. And the second is like it. You shall love your neighbor as yourself. On these two commandments depend all the law and the prophets" (Matthew 22:37–40). Here Jesus clearly makes a connection between the love of God whom we do not see with the love of our neighbor whom we do see. When we love and care for our neighbor, we are loving God. This love is not a selfish love but a sacrificial love and one that keeps on giving. You might be asking yourself, and who is my neighbor? Our neighbor is anyone whom we meet in life and who needs our help. It may be that they need some food, or perhaps they need us to listen to them. It could mean that they need to be encouraged and uplifted, and sometimes it means they might need to be corrected and reprimanded. Regardless of the specific situation, we are supposed to look after the needs of other people before our personal needs. This is how we love with the love of God. It is a selfless and sacrificial love. As Jesus reminds us, "As the Father has loved Me, so have I loved you; abide in My love" (John 15:9). Jesus also raises the

bar for His followers when He tells them that they
are also to love their enemies, "You have heard that it
was said, 'You shall love your neighbor and hate your
enemy.' But I say to you, 'Love your enemies and pray
for those who persecute you, so that you may be sons
of your Father who is in heaven; for He makes the
sun rise on the evil and on the good, and sends rain
on the just and on the unjust'" (Matthew 5:43–45).

All of this is difficult because it goes against our
human nature. Human nature tells us that if someone
hits you, then you hit them back. If they hate you,
then you should hate them back. Yet Jesus tells us that
we cannot do that. The rules of the Kingdom are different, and according to the Gospel of Matthew, they
are very challenging. While on the one hand it is easy
to love family members, close friends, and relatives, it
is much harder to love those whom you do not know
well or who irritate you; the person at work who rat-
tles your nerves, the neighbor whose dog barks all
night long, and so forth. Love, according to the Gospel of Matthew, invites us to go out of our comfort
zones and love our enemies and pray for them.

The Apostle Paul also teaches us about love. In his
first letter to the Corinthians, he gives us a long teach-
ing about the qualities of love. The Corinthian community was divided. There were people who thought
that they were spiritually superior than others in the
community. There was bickering and fighting taking
place. People were not a community of love. There-

fore, Paul needed to address these divisions. Towards
the end of his epistle, Paul delineates for us what love
is, at least in a Christian perspective:

> Love is patient and kind; love is not jealous or
> boastful; it is not arrogant or rude. Love does
> not insist on its own way; it is not irritable or
> resentful; it does not rejoice at wrong, but re-
> joices in the right. Love bears all things, be-
> lieves all things, hopes all things, endures all
> things. Love never ends; as for prophecies, they
> will pass away; as for tongues, they will cease; as
> for knowledge, it will pass away. For our knowl-
> edge is imperfect and our prophecy is imper-
> fect; but when the perfect comes, the imperfect
> will pass away. When I was a child, I spoke like
> a child, I thought like a child, I reasoned like a
> child; when I became a man, I gave up child-
> ish ways. For now we see in a mirror dimly, but
> then face to face. Now I know in part; then I
> shall understand fully, even as I have been fully
> understood. So faith, hope, love abide, these
> three; but the greatest of these is love (1 Cor.
> 13:4–13).

It is helpful to make a list of the words that Paul
uses in this passage in order to see the parameters of
love more clearly:

Love Is:	Love is Not:
Patient	Jealous
Kind	Boastful
Bears all things	Arrogant

Believes	**Rude**
Hope	**Selfish**
Endures	**Resentful**
Never ends	**Rejoices at wrong**
Rejoices in right	

Take some time to review both of these lists. Think of all the times that you thought was love, but really looking at the two lists, realize that it was not love. Love, according to the terms that the Apostle Paul uses is not easy. We can sum up Paul's words by saying that love is always giving. It is gift. The more we learn to love the more we grow:

Today, as we pass the middle of lent,
By the might of the cross
Let us glorify the mighty God and Savior
Who was lifted up in the midst of the earth.
As we look, show us Your sufferings, Master,
And Your precious resurrection,//
Granting us purification and
Great mercy.

Let us humble our fleshly passions
By turning away from food and laying our pleasures aside.
Let us kiss the tree of the cross in faith.
It reveals itself through veneration,
And sanctifies all with divine grace!
So let us sing to the Lord:
We give thanks to You, tender-hearted one,//
For You are saving our souls through the cross!

(*Lord I Call Fourth Monday of Great Lent*)

As we all venerate the cross, let us cry:
Rejoice, tree of life!
Rejoice, holy scepter of Christ!
Rejoice, heavenly glory of man!
Rejoice, majesty of faith!
Rejoice, invincible weapon!
Rejoice, vanquisher of enemies!
Rejoice, shining radiance which saves the world!
Rejoice, great glory of martyrs!
Rejoice, power of saints!
Rejoice, light of the angels!//
Rejoice, precious cross!
(*Lord I call Monday of Fourth Week of Lent*)

FOOD FOR THOUGHT

1. Jesus said that the pure in heart shall see God. Are you trying to be pure in heart? What are the obstacles that get in the way of purity and goodness?

2. It was mentioned that compost is decomposed food, not a pretty image! Yet the spiritual life requires that part of us must die in order for the light of Christ to shine through. What are the things in your life that have to die? How can you live more humbly in your life? How can you better serve others in concrete ways?

3. Do you find yourself to be an impatient person? Are there times when you are more impatient than others? How can you try to become more patient?

4. The Beatles once sang, "All you need is love" and that is very true. Love is the foundation of the Gospel, yet we often fall short of truly loving others. How can you become more loving and caring in your life? How can you help spread love to others? What are some of the obstacles to loving the people around you?

CHAPTER THREE

YEA O LORD AND KING

We have come to the final section of the prayer. The final portion the prayer refers to God as Lord and King, two very common metaphors for God that are found in the Bible. It was mentioned earlier that the terms Lord and Master were originally and more popularly attributed to the Roman Emperor. Yet in the prayer of St. Ephrem, these terms are now attributed to God.

According to the Scriptures, God is also referred to as a judge, creator, and king. There are numerous examples from the Old Testament which refers to God the Father as king:

> The Lord reigns; he is robed in majesty
> The Lord is robed, he is girded with strength.
> Yea, the world is established; it shall never be moved;
> Thy throne is established from of old;
> Thou art from everlasting.
> The floods have lifted up, O Lord,
> The floods have lifted up their voice,

The floods lift up their roaring.
Mightier than the thunders of many waters,
Mightier than the waves of the sea,
The Lord on high is mighty!
Thy decrees are very sure;
Holiness befits thy house,
O Lord, for evermore.
(*Psalm 93*)

The Lord reigns; let the earth rejoice
Let the many coastlands be glad!
Clouds and thick darkness are round about him;
Righteousness and justice are the foundation
of his throne.
Fire goes before him
And burns up his adversaries round about.
His lightnings lighten the world;
The earth sees and trembles.
The mountains melt like wax before the Lord,
Before the Lord of all the earth.
The heavens proclaim his righteousness;
And all the peoples behold his glory.
All worshipers of images are put to shame,
Who make their boast in worthless idols;
All gods bow down before him.
Zion hears and is glad,
And the daughters of Judah rejoice,
Because of thy judgments, O God.
For thou, O Lord, art most high over all the earth;
Thou art exalted far above all gods.
The Lord loves those who hate evil;
He preserves the lives of his saints;
He delivers them from the hand of the wicked.

Light dawns for the righteous,
And joy for the upright in heart.
Rejoice in the Lord, O you righteous,
And give thanks to his holy name!
(*Psalm 96*)

O sing to the Lord a new song,
Or he has done marvelous things!
His right hand and his holy arm
Have gotten him victory.
The Lord has made known his victory,
He has revealed his vindication in the sight of
the nations.
He has remembered his steadfast love and
faithfulness
To the house of Israel.
All the ends of the earth have seen
The victory of our God.
Make a joyful noise to the Lord, all the earth;
Break forth into joyous song and sing praises!
Sing praises to the Lord with the lyre,
with the lyre and the sound of melody!
With trumpets and the sound of the horn
Make a joyful noise before the King, the Lord!
Let the sea roar, and all that fills it;
The world and those who dwell in it!
Let the floods clap their hands;
Let the hills sing for joy together
Before the Lord, for he comes
To judge the earth.
He will judge the world with righteousness,
And the peoples with equity
(*Psalm 98*)

The Lord reigns; let the peoples tremble!
He sits enthroned upon the cherubim; let the
earth quake!
The Lord is great in Zion;
He is exalted over all the peoples.
Let them praise thy great and terrible name!
Holy is he!
Mighty King, lover of justice,
Thou hast established equity;
Thou hast executed justice
And righteousness in Jacob.
Extol the Lord our God;
Worship at his footstool!
Holy is he!
Moses and Aaron were among his priests,
Samuel also was among those who called on
his name.
They cried to the Lord, and he answered them.
He spoke to them in the pillar of cloud;
They kept his testimonies,
And the statutes that he gave them.
O Lord our God, thou didst answer them;
Thou wast a forgiving God to them,
But an avenger of their wrongdoings.
Extol the Lord our God,
And worship at his holy mountain;
For the Lord our God is holy!
(*Psalm 99*)

These Psalms present us with different images of
the king. He is depicted in his royal apparel and seated on his throne. Kings always have a royal chamber

or room which is cared for by a consort of chamber servants, ministers, butlers, and maids. Also, kings usually sit on their throne, which is often raised several steps higher than the rest of the chairs in the room. Other royal symbols are the kingly staff, orb, and crown. In the Scriptures, these royal or kingly attributes are attributed to God. Earthly kings may seem to have power but it is nothing compared to the power of God.

God's kingly and royal attributes are also attributed to Jesus. The Gospel of Matthew opens with the birth narratives. Here, the Magi or wise men come to worship the Christ child. They ascertained from the stars that the Messiah was to be born in Bethlehem. They tell Herod that they have come to pay homage to the king. This news sends King Herod into a rage and he later wants to have all the newborn children killed in order to destroy anyone who might challenge his authority. He is the sole ruler of the Jews:

> Now when Jesus was born in Bethlehem of Judea in the days of Herod the king, behold, wise men from the East came to Jerusalem, saying, "Where is he who has been born king of the Jews? For we have seen his star in the East, and have come to worship him." When Herod the king heard this, he was troubled, and all Jerusalem with him; and assembling all the chief priests and scribes of the people, he inquired of them where the Christ was to be born. They told him, "In Bethlehem of Judea; for so it is

written by the prophet: 'And you, O Bethlehem, in the land of Judah, are by no means
least among the rulers of Judah; for from you
shall come a ruler who will govern my people
Israel.' "Then Herod summoned the wise men
secretly and ascertained from them what time
the star appeared; and he sent them to Bethlehem, saying, "Go and search diligently for the
child, and when you have found him bring me
word, that I too may come and worship him."
When they had heard the king they went their
way; and lo, the star which they had seen in the
East went before them, till it came to rest over
the place where the child was. When they saw
the star, they rejoiced exceedingly with great
joy; and going into the house they saw the child
with Mary his mother, and they fell down and
worshiped him. Then, opening their treasures,
they offered him gifts, gold and frankincense
and myrrh. And being warned in a dream not
to return to Herod, they departed to their own
country by another way (Matthew 2:1–12).

In the Gospel of John, we have a public affir-
mation and confirmation of Jesus as both Lord and
King. In the very beginning of the Gospel, Jesus calls
His disciples and when He meets Philip and Nathaniel they follow Him. Nathaniel proclaims that Jesus is
both Son of God and King of Israel. Later in the same
Gospel, when Jesus is crucified, Pontius Pilate makes
sure to have Jesus' title on the sign or placard above
the cross — Jesus of Nazareth the King of the Jews:

The next day Jesus decided to go to Galilee. And he found Philip and said to him, "Follow me." Now Philip was from Beth-sa'ida, the city of Andrew and Peter.

Philip found Nathan'ael, and said to him, "We have found him of whom Moses in the law and also the prophets wrote, Jesus of Nazareth, the son of Joseph." Nathan'ael said to him, "Can anything good come out of Nazareth?" Philip said to him, "Come and see." Jesus saw Nathan'ael coming to him, and said of him, "Behold, an Israelite indeed, in whom is no guile!" Nathanel said to him, "How do you know me?" Jesus answered him, "Before Philip called you, when you were under the fig tree, I saw you." Nathan'ael answered him, "Rabbi, you are the Son of God! You are the King of Israel!" Jesus answered him, "Because I said to you, I saw you under the fig tree, do you believe? You shall see greater things than these." And he said to him, "Truly, truly, I say to you, you will see heaven opened, and the angels of God ascending and descending upon the Son of man."
(John 1:35–51)

Upon this Pilate sought to release him, but the Jews cried out, "If you release this man, you are not Caesar's friend; every one who makes himself a king sets himself against Caesar." When Pilate heard these words, he brought Jesus out and sat down on the judgment seat at a place called The Pavement, and in Hebrew, Gab'batha. Now it was the day of Preparation of the Passover; it was about the sixth hour. He said to the Jews, "Behold your King!" They cried out, "Away with him, away with him, crucify him!" Pilate said to them, "Shall I crucify your King?" The chief priests answered, "We have no king but Caesar." Then he handed him over to them to be crucified. So they took Jesus, and he went out, bearing his own cross, to the place called the place of a skull, which is called in Hebrew Gol'gotha. There they crucified him, and with him two others, one on either side, and Jesus between them. Pilate also wrote a title and put it on the cross; it read, "Jesus of Nazareth, the King of the Jews." Many of the Jews read this title, for the place where Jesus was crucified was near the city; and it was written in Hebrew, in Latin, and in Greek. The chief priests of the Jews then said to Pilate, "Do not write, 'The King of the Jews,' but, 'This man said, I am King of the Jews.'" Pilate answered, "What I have written I have written." (John 19:12–22)

In the first petition in the prayer, we address God as Lord and King and ask Him to help us see our own sins, which is a very difficult thing to do. Very often we do not see ourselves in the same light as our spouse, children, or neighbors. Sometimes we are oblivious. If we are lucky, our husband or wife will make sure these things are made known to us, often in not so nice ways! It is important to sit down and look at your life in truthfulness and honesty, taking an account of the relationships with family, friends, neighbors, and co-workers. This process is called the examination of conscience and it is a healthy practice.

The Church gives us the sacrament of confession as a way to help us take account of our sins. Confession is an examination of conscience. Confession helps us look at ourselves in light of the Gospel so that we can see where we have fallen short of loving other people. Sins can be identified in two major categories, sins of commission and sins of omission. The sins of commission are things that we do that hurt other people, such as not paying attention to family members when they are speaking or spending time with your children when they need help. Sins of omission are when we overlook the needs of other people. For example, your neighbor might be in need, perhaps his wife is dealing with cancer and the other people in the Home Owners Association are taking turns to make meals for them and cutting the grass. If you are oblivious to the needs of your neighbor and do not help them, you are committing a sin of omission. Basically, you are not loving your neighbor as you should. Below are several questions for reflection to assist with your examination of conscience. Sit down in a quiet place, perhaps a quiet place in your house or maybe take a walk outside, and think about your life. Some people practice an examination of conscience daily, weekly, or monthly. At minimum, I would hope that you use these questions before participating in the sacrament of confession. Some people choose to keep a spiritual journal where you list your sins or shortcomings. You can list the ways in which you are deepening your faith in Christ:

Questions for Examination:
1. Are you always loving and caring towards your spouse, children, family members, neighbors, and friends?
2. Do you put your neighbors needs in front of your needs?
3. Do you give generously of your time, talent, and treasure, or are you stingy and greedy?
4. Do you seek the good in all things or do you seek after your own wishes?
5. Are you living a good Christian life as an example for your family?
6. Do your actions follow your words? In other words do you walk the walk of faith rather than just talking about it?
7. Do you participate fully in the life of the Church?
8. Do you read the Scriptures regularly and try to learn more about the Word of God?
9. Are you an agent of peace with the people around you?
10. Do you try to forgive other people?

Spiritual inventories are a good part of our preparation for Confession and Holy Communion. In his epistle to the Corinthians, Paul tells his congregation that before coming to the Lord's Table that they should examine themselves before partaking of the Body and Blood of Christ (1 Corinthians 11:23–32). This means that we should examine our conscience for any wrongdoing against others. The more we engage in this activity the more we will begin to understand how our life impacts other people and how their lives impact us.

J UDGING. The final petition and conclusion to this prayer is asking God for the strength not to judge our brothers or sisters, something that is easy to say, but hard to do. Judging others is a big obstacle which is difficult to overcome. It is very easy to look around and point our finger at other people. We might criticize our neighbors. We might judge the neighbor who does not volunteer during the monthly Home Owners Association work days. The list can go on *ad infinitum*. When we judge other people, we are setting ourselves up as the judge. We judge others for the clothes that they wear, how they speak, how they look. We judge them based on the color of their skin, their religious beliefs, or their education. We judge people based on how they spend their money. Every day we are tempted to judge people.

You might think that going to church helps prevent judging people, but it does not. Sometimes going to church makes it even easier to judge people.

We see people coming late to Church. We hear them
sing off key. We see the clothes they are wearing. We
overhear gossip at coffee hour. The list is long. It is
highly appropriate that the prayer of St. Ephrem concludes with the sin of judging others.

The Scriptures include harsh statements about
judging other people. According to the Bible, only
God the Father is the judge. All power and authority rests with Him. All of Jesus' power and authority
comes from God. Below are a few examples from the
Old Testament about judging:

> O Lord my God, in thee do I take refuge;
> Save me from all my pursuers, and deliver me,
> Lest like a lion they rend me,
> Dragging me away, with none to rescue.
> O Lord my God, if I have done this,
> If there is wrong in my hands,
> If I have requited my friend with evil
> Or plundered my enemy without cause,
> Let the enemy pursue me and overtake me,
> And let him trample my life to the ground,
> And lay my soul in the dust. [Selah]
> Arise, O Lord, in thy anger,
> Lift thyself up against the fury of my enemies;
> Awake, O my God; thou hast appointed a judgment.
> Let the assembly of the peoples be gathered
> about thee;
> And over it take thy seat on high.
> The Lord judges the peoples;
> Judge me, O Lord, according to my righteousness
> And according to the integrity that is in me.

O let the evil of the wicked come to an end,
But establish thou the righteous,
Thou who triest the minds and hearts,
Thou righteous God.
My shield is with God,
Who saves the upright in heart.
God is a righteous judge,
And a God who has indignation every day
(Psalm 7:1–11)

But the Lord sits enthroned for ever,
He has established his throne for judgment;
And he judges the world with righteousness,
He judges the peoples with equity.
The Lord is a stronghold for the oppressed,
A stronghold in times of trouble.
And those who know thy name put their trust
in thee,
For thou, O Lord, hast not forsaken those who
seek thee.
Sing praises to the Lord, who dwells in Zion!
Tell among the peoples his deeds!
For he who avenges blood is mindful of them;
He does not forget the cry of the afflicted
(Psalm 9:7–11)

We give thanks to thee, O God; we give thanks;
We call on thy name and recount thy wondrous deeds.
At the set time which I appoint
I will judge with equity.
When the earth totters, and all its inhabitants,
It is I who keep steady its pillars. [Selah]
I say to the boastful, "Do not boast,"

And to the wicked, "Do not lift up your horn;
Do not lift up your horn on high,
Or speak with insolent neck."
For not from the east or from the west
And not from the wilderness comes lifting up;
But it is God who executes judgment,
Putting down one and lifting up another.
For in the hand of the Lord there is a cup,
With foaming wine, well mixed;
And he will pour a draught from it,
And all the wicked of the earth
Shall drain it down to the dregs.
But I will rejoice for ever,
I will sing praises to the God of Jacob.
All the horns of the wicked he will cut off,
But the horns of the righteous shall be exalted
(Psalm 75)

These are just a few examples from the Psalms that speak about God's authority as judge. God is a judge who judges justly. He is fair and merciful despite the fact that we disobey Him time and time again. Thankfully, He is a loving and caring God, a God who wants us to repent and change our life for the better. It is important that we do not judge other people, that is not our business! Our business is to be about our Father's business of loving and caring for creation, for serving Him, and for loving our neighbors.

Jesus highlights the message of judgment in the story of the Publican and the Pharisee. The Publican is a tax collector, a Jew who was working for the Romans. The Romans hired tax collectors to collect various types of taxes in the Empire, for wars, roads, and buildings. Taxes helped the Romans expand the Empire and build a vast network of communication, including highways, buildings, and seaports. Some tax collectors in the New Testament are mentioned by name, such as Levi who later had his name changed to Matthew, and Zachaeus who Luke tells us climbed up a sycamore tree in order to see Jesus pass through Jericho. This particular Publican is unnamed, yet from what Luke tells us, we can see his sincerity in his repentance. All he said was "have mercy on me a sinner."

The Pharisee, however, was praying to God and comparing himself to the Publican:

> He also told this parable to some who trusted in themselves that they were righteous and despised others: "Two men went up into the temple to pray, one a Pharisee and the other a tax collector. The Pharisee stood and prayed thus with himself, 'God, I thank Thee that I am not like other men, extortioners, unjust, adulterers, or even like this tax collector. I fast twice a week, I give tithes of all that I get.' But the tax collector, standing far off, would not even lift up his eyes to heaven, but beat his breast, saying, 'God, be merciful to me a sinner!' I tell you, this man went down to his house justified rather than the other; for every one who exalts himself will be humbled, but he who humbles himself will be exalted" (Luke 18:9–14).

"Judge not, that you be not judged. For with the judgment you pronounce you will be judged, and the measure you give will be the measure you get. Why do you see the speck that is in your brother's eye, but do not notice the log that is in your own eye? Or how can you say to your brother, 'Let me take the speck out of your eye,' when there is the log in your own eye? You hypocrite, first take the log out of your own eye, and then you will see clearly to take the speck out of your brother's eye" (Matthew 7:1–5).

"When the Son of man comes in His glory, and all the angels with Him, then He will sit on His glorious throne. Before Him will be gathered all the nations, and He will separate them one from another as a shepherd separates the sheep from the goats, and He will place the sheep at His right hand, but the goats at the left. Then the King will say to those at his right hand, 'Come, O blessed of My Father, inherit the kingdom prepared for you from the foundation of the world; for I was hungry and you gave Me food, I was thirsty and you gave Me drink, I was a stranger and you welcomed Me, I was naked and you clothed Me, I was sick and you visited Me, I was in prison and you came to Me.' Then the righteous will answer Him, 'Lord, when did we see Thee hungry and feed Thee, or thirsty and give Thee drink? And when did we see Thee a stranger and welcome Thee, or naked and clothe Thee? And when did we see Thee sick or in prison and visit Thee?' And the King will answer them, 'Truly, I say to you, as you did it to one of the least of these My brethren, you did it to Me.' Then He will say to those at His left hand, 'Depart from Me, you cursed, into the eternal fire prepared for the devil and his angels; for I was hungry and you gave Me no food, I was thirsty and you gave Me no drink, I was a stranger and you did not welcome Me, naked and you did not clothe Me, sick and in prison and you did not visit Me.' Then they also will answer, 'Lord, when did we see Thee hungry or thirsty or a stranger or naked or sick or in prison, and did not minister to Thee?' Then He will answer them, 'Truly, I say to you, as you did it not to one of the least of these, you did it not to Me.' And they will go away into eternal punishment, but the righteous into eternal life" (Matt. 25:36–46).

The last Scripture selection above is from the Gospel of Matthew, which also is read on the last Sunday before the beginning of Great Lent. Jesus teaches us about the true nature of repentance, the love of the neighbor. Here, in this long passage, we see that Jesus highlights six things that are repeated four times in this lesson:

Feeding the hungry
Drink for the thirsty
Visiting the prisoners
Visiting the sick
Clothing the naked
Welcoming the stranger

These six qualities are the foundation of our Lenten journey. Lent can sometimes be a selfish rather than selfless time of year. We tend to focus on foods that we can or cannot eat, or how many liturgical services we attend or do not attend. We lose track of the real reason for Lent, which is repentance and changing our life. Lent is not meant for us to focus on ourselves, but on the needy neighbor who requires our love and attention. The prophets highlighted the major problems in Israel: neglecting the poor, orphans, widows, homeless, hungry, and imprisoned. The kings of Israel did not take care of the people. They did not care for those who needed help. The rulers of Israel did not follow God's will. Time after time God raised up prophets like Hosea, Amos, Jeremiah, and Isaiah to call Israel to repentance. They called for a fast, but not just a fast from certain types of food, but a fast that would change Israel's attitude towards God. The true fast is caring for the neighbor as we see in this final scriptural selection from Isaiah. Let this Scripture be our motto for Great Lent and which best encapsulates the message of St. Ephrem's prayer:

> "Is not this the fast that I choose:
> To loose the bonds of wickedness,
> To undo the thongs of the yoke,
> To let the oppressed go free,
> And to break every yoke?
> Is it not to share your bread with the hungry,
> And bring the homeless poor into your house;

When you see the naked, to cover him,
And not to hide yourself from your own flesh?
Then shall your light break forth like the dawn,
And your healing shall spring up speedily;
Your righteousness shall go before you,
The glory of the Lord shall be your rear guard.
Then you shall call, and the Lord will answer;
You shall cry, and he will say, Here I am."
If you take away from the midst of you the yoke,
The pointing of the finger, and speaking wickedness,
If you pour yourself out for the hungry
And satisfy the desire of the afflicted,
Then shall your light rise in the darkness
And your gloom be as the noonday.
And the Lord will guide you continually,
And satisfy your desire with good things,
And make your bones strong;
And you shall be like a watered garden,
Like a spring of water,
Whose waters fail not.
And your ancient ruins shall be rebuilt;
You shall raise up the foundations of many
generations;
You shall be called the repairer of the breach,
The restorer of streets to dwell in (Is. 58:4–9).

FOOD FOR THOUGHT

1. The final portion of St. Ephrem's Prayer begins
    with calling God both Lord and Master. What
    are some of the false gods and idols in your life
    that you worship? What are the things in life that
    take your attention away from God as your Lord
    and Master?

2. Do you go to confession regularly throughout
    the year? Confession is a good way to acknowl-
    edge the sins in your life? Before participating in
    confession take some quiet time alone and think
    about all the different relationships in your life;
    with your spouse, parents, children, friends, co-
    workers, and neighbors. Are you at peace with
    everyone? Do you love everyone or do you har-
    bor ill will towards them?

3. Jesus warns us against judging other people. Judg-
    ing others however is a great and grave tempta-
    tion. Take some time and reflect on the times
    when you have judged other people? Why do you
    judge them? If we become more loving towards
    other people we will tend to love them more and
    not judge them because in loving them we realize
    our own sinfulness and brokenness.

BIBLIOGRAPHY

BOOKS ON ST. EPHREM THE SYRIAN

Brock, Sebastian (introd. and trans.). *St. Ephrem the Syrian Hymns on Paradise*. Crestwood, NY: St. Vladimir's Seminary Press, 1990.

Clement, Oliver. *Three Prayers: The Lord's Prayer, O Heavenly King, Prayer of St. Ephrem*. Crestwood, NY: St. Vladimir's Seminary Press, 2000.

Griffith, Sidney. *Faith Adoring the Mystery: Reading the Bible with St. Ephrem the Syrian*. Marquette, WI: Marquette University Press, 1997.

Hansbury, Mary. *Hymns of St. Ephrem the Syrian*. Collegeville, MN: Cistercian Publications, 2007.

McVey, Kathleen (intro. and trans.). *St. Ephrem the Syrian*. Mahwah, NJ: Paulist Press, 1989.

DESERT MOTHERS AND FATHERS

Chitty, Derwas. *The Desert A City*. Crestwood: St. Vladimir's Seminary Press, 1995.

Chrysavgis, John. *In the Heart of the Desert: The Spirituality of the Desert Fathers and Mothers*. Bloomington, IN, 2003.

Keller, David. *Oasis of Wisdom: The Worlds of the Desert Fathers and Mothers*. Collegeville, MN: Liturgical Press, 2005.

Nouwen, Henry. *The Way of the Heart: Desert Spirituality and Contemporary Ministry*. San Francisco: HaperSanFrancisco, 1981.

Swan, Laura. *The Forgotten Desert Mothers: Sayings, Lives, and Stories of Early Christian Women*. New York: Paulist Press, 2001.

Ward, Benedicta. *The Sayings of the Desert Fathers: The Alphabetical Collection*. Kalamazoo: Cistercian Publications, 1975.

RESOURCES FOR GREAT LENT

Hopko, Thomas. *The Lenten Spring*. Crestwood, NY: St. Vladimir's Seminary Press, 1983.

Mills, William C. *Let Us Attend: Reflections on the Gospel of Mark for the Lenten Season*. Rollinsford, NH: Orthodox Research Institute, 2008.

Schmemann, Alexander. *Great Lent: Journey to Pascha*. Crestwood, NY: St. Vladimir's Seminary Press, 1969.

_____. *Celebration of Faith: The Church Year Ser-*

mons. Volume 2. Crestwood, NY: St. Vladimir's Seminary Press, 1994.

Wybrew, Hugh. *Orthodox Lent, Holy Week, and Easter: Liturgical Texts with Commentary.* Crestwood, NY: St. Vladimir's Seminary Press, 1997.

ABOUT THE AUTHOR

Fr. William Mills, Ph.D., is the rector of the Nativity of the Holy Virgin Orthodox Church in Charlotte, NC. Fr. Mills received his Bachelor of History from Millersville University of Pennsylvania and then pursued theological studies at Saint Vladimir's Orthodox Theological Seminary in Crestwood, NY, where he received his Master of Divinity and Master of Theology degrees. He then pursued advanced theological studies at the Union Institute and University in Cincinnati, Ohio, where he received his doctorate in Pastoral Theology. Fr. Mills is the author of several commentaries on the Gospel readings of the liturgical year, including *Feasts of Faith: Reflections on the Major Feast Days* (Rollinsford, NH: Orthodox Research Institute, 2008). Fr. Mills is available for parish and clergy retreats. Visit his website at www.williamcmills.com.

www.ingramcontent.com/pod-product-compliance
Lightning Source LLC
Chambersburg PA
CBHW020950030426
42339CB00004B/34